Our Father

Harnessing the Power of the Lord's Prayer

Pastor David Scharf

Published by Straight Talk Books
P.O. Box 301, Milwaukee, WI 53201
800.661.3311 • timeofgrace.org

Scripture is taken from THE HOLY BIBLE, NEW INTERNATIONAL VERSION®.
NIV®. Copyright © 1973, 1978, 1984, 2011 by Biblica, Inc.® Used by permission.
All rights reserved worldwide.

Printed in the United States of America
ISBN: 978-1-942107-05-7

Contents

Introduction

*"Cast your cares on the L*ORD
and he will sustain you;
he will never let the righteous fall"
(Psalm 55:22). Amen.

Matthew 6:9-13 says, **"Our Father in heaven, hallowed be your name, your kingdom come, your will be done, on earth as it is in heaven. Give us today our daily bread. And forgive us our debts, as we also have forgiven our debtors. And lead us not into temptation, but deliver us from the evil one."**

This is the prayer Jesus gave us to pray—the Lord's Prayer. What a beautiful prayer, huh? So what did you just pray for? Did you *pray* it or just merely *say* it?

That's not a new temptation for us. There was a monk in the Middle Ages—his name was Bernard of Clairvaux. He was talking to one of his friends, and he was so upset because every time he started praying the Lord's Prayer, he would start thinking about other things. His friend said, "You just need to try a little harder, Bernard. This isn't that hard! Just concentrate." So Bernard bet him his horse. He said, "I'll bet you my horse that you can't say the Lord's Prayer without letting another thought intrude in your mind." The man said, "I'll take that bet!" He cleared his mind, took a deep breath, and started: "Our Father in heaven, hallowed be your name. . . . So does the saddle come with the horse?"

It's hard to do, isn't it? It's why we teach our kids

4

to fold their hands so that their hands don't "get distracted." It's why we teach them to close their eyes when they pray so that their eyes won't get distracted. But what do we do so that our *minds* don't get distracted? Because if we drone through this prayer week in and week out thousands of times throughout our lives but never think about it, we are no more communicating with God any more than I am communicating with my wife when I nod my head in agreement with what she is saying even though I am thinking about something else (merely hypothetical—never happens, of course).

So to help you and me keep our minds focused, we are going to slow down and really think about the blessings that Jesus gives us in this perfect prayer we call the Lord's Prayer. We'll look at each phrase devotionally. It's important to take time for this because the devil knows how much damage is done when our prayer lives flourish. May God bless our meditation, and may he make us bold to pray!

Our Father in Heaven

What is the most important phrase in the Lord's Prayer? There's no right answer to that question. You could make an argument for all of them. However, I think I can make a fairly strong argument for the phrase before us right now: "Our Father in heaven." I believe it to be the most important phrase of the prayer because without it, none of the rest of the prayer is possible. The reason I say that is because . . .

Prayer is all about RELATIONSHIP.

Let's for a moment imagine that you're going to try to call the White House and speak to the president of the United States. You call and say, "I'd like to speak to the president." What do you suppose the person on the other end of the line would tell you? "He's in a meeting with several presidents of other countries, but hold for a moment and I'll put you right through." No way! There's no way you're going to speak directly to the president. Why not? Because he doesn't know you. You have no relationship with him. Now what if your name was Baron or Tiffany or Malia or Sasha? You would get right through! Every time. Because he's your father.

Prayer works the same way; it's all about relationship. Prayer is a privilege that only God's children have. I know it sounds strange to hear that only believers can pray and be heard, but it's what God's Word says: **"But your iniquities have separated you from your God; your sins have hidden his face from you, so that *he will not hear*"** (Isaiah 59:2). It's not that God can't hear;

it's that he won't hear those who are not his children.

And yet, Jesus tells us that when we call out to the One who flings stars into space and measures the universe with the span of his hand and confines the mighty oceans in their channels, we can call him Father. And he'll listen. Why? It's because through Jesus and because of Jesus we have that relationship with God.

We can call him Father, and he'll listen.

"But when the set time had fully come, God sent his Son, born of a woman, born under law, to redeem those under law, that we might receive adoption to sonship" (Galatians 4:4,5). Why can you pray? Because by his life and death on a cross, Jesus has made God *your* Father.

And yet, notice that Jesus didn't teach us to pray, "*My* Father in heaven" but "*Our* Father in heaven."

God is OUR Father.

Have you noticed that this prayer that Jesus teaches us is plural: "*Our* Father," "give *us* today *our* daily bread," "forgive *us our* debts, as *we* also have forgiven *our* debtors," "lead *us* not into temptation, but deliver *us* from the evil one." That's nine plural pronouns. Our private prayers tend to be like this: "Give me, bless me, etc." And there's nothing wrong with that, but Jesus wants you to remember not only the comfort that you have a relationship with God but that you are part of a family with lots of brothers and sisters in Christ all around the world. This is a prayer not just for *my* needs, but for *our* needs.

So often we ask people to keep us in their prayers when something challenging happens or even when something joyful happens. Or we'll request a special prayer in church so that the whole congregation is praying. And that's such a comfort to know that people are praying for you and with you. But think about this: before the sun sets around the globe today, millions of prayers will be prayed to the God of all grace on your behalf, prayed by Christians who speak the "our Father in heaven."

And finally, that's not insignificant to recognize when you pray that . . .

Our Father is IN HEAVEN.

Maybe this concept of viewing God as Father is not a particularly comforting thought because you still have "dad scars" that run deep. Truthfully, we will all struggle a bit with this, because even if you had a great father, you didn't have a perfect father who loved you perfectly. I certainly know my failings as a father. As hard as I might try, there are places that earthly love can't travel and problems that my love can't solve and mistakes that my love makes.

And that's what makes this thought tough for many, because the truth is that every human being gets affirmation from his or her father. Little boys in Little League are looking for *their* dads in the stands. They don't care who else is there—they need to see *their* fathers. A little girl wearing a dress loves to hear Mom say how beautiful she looks, but she needs to show Daddy so that he can make her day by saying,

"You look so pretty!" Every earthly father fails in this sometimes. Sometimes earthly fathers just aren't there.

But our Father is *in heaven.* He never fails to give you the affirmation and the confidence you need. Our Father in heaven loves to remind you: "You are my perfect child because of Jesus. I will never stop loving you. I loved you so much I gave my Son to die on a cross for you. I will never let you go. You just go ahead and ask me for anything; I'll give it to you. I forgave you yesterday, I forgive you today, and I'll forgive you tomorrow. You are my child, and nothing will change that."

Oh, and because he's in heaven, it means that everything you see around you is owned by your Father—he can back up what he says. That ought to make you bold to pray as Jesus taught you!

O God, through Jesus' sacrifice you have restored us as your forgiven children. In his name make us bold to pray: Our Father in heaven. Amen.

Hallowed Be Your Name

Does it seem a little silly to pray that God's name be kept holy? Isn't that a little like asking that water be wet or tigers be carnivorous? Here's the key: in this phrase we're asking that God's name be kept holy by us!

So what is God's name? Well, God's name is everything he reveals about who he is and what he does. Want proof? What do you think of when I say the name Tom Cruise? You don't just think of his face. It's more than that—you think of everything you know about him—all the movies he's in, who he's been married to, how weird he is . . . and that brings us right to an important point. A good name can be tarnished. God's name is perfectly holy in itself. Like pure gold is 24 carat—you can't make 26-carat gold—it can't get more pure. What is the only thing you can do? You can dilute it to make 18-carat or 14-carat gold. In this phrase, we are praying that we don't dilute God's name but keep it holy. How do we do that?

God's name is everything he reveals about who he is and what he does.

God's name is kept holy when we TEACH IT PURELY.

If you've ever talked with someone who is interviewed often for newspapers, he or she might say you can't believe everything you read because the reporter picks and chooses what to share of the interview. Misquoting someone can totally change how you view that person. God's name is no different—he doesn't like to be misquoted!

With this phrase we're praying for churches to hold to all of God's truth and not just some of it. We're praying for pastors and teachers to have the courage to proclaim all that God says and not shy away from difficult conversations. But let's bring it down to a more personal level—to our everyday lives. It's easy to misquote our Father in heaven, sometimes without even realizing it.

You've maybe heard it said, "Children seldom misquote you. They more often repeat word for word what you shouldn't have said." That's not God's problem with his children—we sometimes get it wrong without even trying. It's easy to change "love your enemies" to "love your allies." It's easy to change "trust in the Lord with all your heart" to "trust in the Lord with just a part." It's so tempting to be like the little boy who said, "A lie is an abomination to the Lord, but an ever-present help in trouble." It's tempting to change "godliness with contentment is great gain" into "great gain will lead to godly contentment."

And yet, aren't you glad that God has revealed that he covers you with his holiness in your baptism and places his holy name on you? Aren't you glad that your salvation is not dependent on you but solely on the sacrifice of Jesus on the cross? So am I.

Now as forgiven children of God, you and I not only pray that we teach God's Word purely, but that we realize that . . .

God's name is kept holy when we LIVE IT RIGHTLY.

I'm talking to the kids with this one (parents read too!). Imagine that a nice family moved next door to you. Your parents want them to feel welcome, and so your two families go to a baseball game. While you are at the game, you start throwing pieces of your hot pretzel at the back of people's heads. When your parents tell you to stop, you snap back at them, "I can do what I want!"

First, you should be embarrassed! But your parents would also be embarrassed. Why? Because your behavior is a reflection on them and how they raised you. Now imagine that your parents proceed to invite your neighbors to check out your church. As a selling point, they mention how you've learned good Christian values and manners there. How likely do you think it would be that your neighbors will check out your church?

The loudest sermon people will ever hear is your life.

I think you get the point. The loudest sermon people will ever hear is your life. Make it one that draws people to their Savior. Make it one that is so good that others see your good deeds and glorify God. Make it one that gives glory to Jesus, no matter who is watching. Make it one that hallows God's name.

O Father, help us to know you through your inspired Word and to live by it as children in your family. In Jesus' name make us bold to pray: Hallowed be your name. Amen.

Your Kingdom Come

With the exception of the ones in existence now, every kingdom has fallen. And maybe you say, "duh!" But that ought to make us think. History repeats itself. It appears to be in the nature of kingdoms, at least earthly ones, to fall. There have been some pretty great ones that people thought would be around forever. Before Christ, talk with the Egyptians, the Babylonians, the Persians, the Greeks—all of them would have told you that their kingdoms would last forever. During Jesus' time, ask the Romans how long they would last, and they would have told you forever! It's interesting that historians have credited Rome's fall to the increase of divorce, increase of taxes for social programs, sports mania, crippling military costs, and the decay of religion. Thankfully that will never be America! Ahem.

We thank God for our country. We thank God for those who fought for our freedoms. But most important, we thank God for the freedom we have in our country to proclaim God's truth and ask him to continue to provide that freedom. Not many countries have that freedom, and it is a special blessing. We also realize, though, that this country will likely go the way of every other kingdom on earth. But in this part of the Lord's Prayer, we pray for one kingdom that will never come to an end: Jesus' kingdom.

What is Jesus' kingdom? Well, the word *kingdom* is literally the "king's dominion." What does Jesus have dominion over? Everything! And that's true. But when we pray "your kingdom come," we're not praying that Jesus would set up shop visibly on earth in the form of a kingdom. Jesus told Pilate, **"My kingdom is not of this world"** (John 18:36). Jesus told the religious leaders, **"The kingdom of God is not something that can be observed, nor will people say, 'Here it is,' or 'There it is,' because the kingdom of God is in your midst"** (Luke 17:20,21). Jesus' kingdom is his rule in hearts through his Word. So . . .

"Your kingdom come" is a prayer for MY HEART.

I was born a citizen of the United States of America, and I have a birth certificate to prove it. But what does it take to be a citizen in Jesus' kingdom? That doesn't come by birth certificate but by baptism certificate. When Jesus worked faith in your heart through Baptism or through the Word, you, no matter if you were in America or Germany or Brazil or Timbuktu, became a citizen of Jesus' kingdom. The devil who only wants to destroy you like a roaring lion was cast out as king of your heart, and Jesus has taken his place. "Your kingdom come" is a prayer to keep Jesus there.

Jesus' kingdom is his rule in hearts through his Word.

Here's the thing: it's sometimes tough to believe that God's answering this prayer. Tell me if this isn't you sometimes. You know what Jesus did on the cross. You know how thankful you are for that. But you know your sin. You know your past. And you wonder, "Is Jesus even for me? Does he still rule in my heart?" I struggle with that sometimes.

The reformer Martin Luther had an interesting illustration to show how silly that thinking is. Imagine that the richest king in the world is so pleased with you that he says, "Ask for anything that you want, and I'll give it to you." And you proceed to ask for a bowl of soup. Wouldn't the king be a little shocked at how little you asked for since he's capable of giving so much more? The same goes with this phrase, "your kingdom come." We ask for no small thing, but God who owns and controls all things, who loved you enough to give you his Son to pay for your sins, now says, "Ask me and I'll give it to you." And so we pray "your kingdom come," knowing that as he rules us through his Word, he answers that prayer. But it's not just for your heart . . .

"Your kingdom come" is a prayer for THE HEARTS OF OTHERS.

This is a missions prayer. We're not praying for Jesus to bring about a physical world domination, but rather a spiritual heart domination. We pray "your kingdom come" every time a baby is baptized; "your kingdom come" whenever someone makes an effort to tell his or her neighbors about Jesus; "your kingdom come" each time our children sing in church and people who aren't normally in church hear the message of Jesus through the lips of children; "your kingdom come" every time we put an offering in a plate, because Jesus uses that money to extend his kingdom here and for missions around the world.

This is a prayer for Jesus to extend his rule into the

hearts of others . . . through you and me. I get to visit numerous churches to talk with the members about their church. I'll often hear people say something along the lines of, "I love my church because we have a mission mind-set." When you ask what they mean, they say, "Because we don't just *talk* missions; we *do* missions." Let's be a church that "does missions." Let's pray boldly that Jesus' kingdom come into the hearts of others through us.

This is a prayer for Jesus to extend his rule into the hearts of others.

O Father, give us your Holy Spirit to rule in our hearts, and use us to extend your kingdom of grace to others. In Jesus' name make us bold to pray: Your kingdom come. Amen.

Your Will Be Done

Be careful of what you ask for; you might just get it. Have you ever heard those words of wisdom before—when someone really wanted you to think about what you were saying? Growing up, when I told my parents that I wanted lots of kids just like them, they could have said, "Be careful of what you ask for; you might just get it." (I come from a family of 14 children!)

I think that's appropriate advice for when we pray, "Your will be done." Someone could rightly say, "Be careful of what you ask for; you might just get it." That's true because . . .

God's will is not always OUR WILL.

What do you want from this life? As Christians, we of course echo the words of the psalmist: **"One thing I ask from the Lord, this only do I seek: that I may dwell in the house of the Lord all the days of my life"** (Psalm 27:4). The one thing I want as a Christian is to be in God's house, in his family, in his presence. But let me be honest; is that really the *one thing* I want? Don't get me wrong; I really do want that, but in the words of Frank Sinatra, I want to do it *my way.*

You pray and pray for Mom to recover. But that's not what happens. She just gets worse. And you wonder, "God, how could you let this happen?" You cry out to God from a worried bed, "God, I don't get why you would've let me lose my job—especially now when I needed it so much!" You struggle with money and pain and relationships and a thousand other problems and think, "How could a loving God let this happen? How could this be his will for my life?"

And there are powerful voices that answer. The world says, "See, God doesn't have the answer." The devil whispers, "See, God doesn't love you like I love you." Your own sin-filled heart chimes in, "See, you can't trust a God who doesn't always give you what you want."

One thing you and I need to understand is what God tells us through the prophet Isaiah: **"As the heavens are higher than the earth, so are my ways higher than your ways and my thoughts than your thoughts"** (Isaiah 55:9). Can you admit that? That your knowledge in any given situation doesn't even come close to full knowledge? I'm reminded of a cartoon of a man walking down the street. He gets hit in the head with a rock. He yells at God, "How could you let this happen?" But in the background you can see Jesus holding back thousands of stones. If you and I could only see all the ways that God withholds vicious attacks in our lives!

God forgive us for praying, "Your will be done . . . so long as it doesn't interfere with my will." Because we can't have it both ways. In the end, there are only two kinds of people in this world: those who say to God, "Your will be done," and those to whom God says in the end, "Your will be done." I want to be the first kind. And it helps to be the first kind when you understand what God's will is. Contrary to popular opinion, God doesn't just want you to be happy. No, God wants something so much greater for you. . . .

God's will is FOR YOU TO BE IN HEAVEN.

The Bible couldn't make that fact more clear: **"This is good, and pleases God our Savior, who wants all people to be saved and to come to a knowledge of the truth"** (1 Timothy 2:3,4). Or as Peter puts it in answering our questions about God's will: **"The Lord is not slow in keeping his promise, as some understand slowness. Instead he is patient with you, not wanting anyone to perish, but everyone to come to repentance"** (2 Peter 3:9). Dear Reader, you are part of the "all" and the "anyone" and the "everyone." God's will is for you to be in heaven!

That means that whatever he needs to do or let happen, he is willing to do in order to keep you in line for heaven, even if that means pain or sickness or death. No one likes enduring those things, but if God deems them necessary to keep you out of hell's courts, then so be it! It's like learning the value of vaccinations. No one likes to get stuck with a needle. But the needle is nothing compared to the disease it prevents!

God's will is for you to be in heaven!

Think this through from a logical perspective. If we always get what we want, when would we and our loved ones ever get to heaven? There would be no sickness, no pain, no tears, no death if we had our way! Sound familiar? That's God's description of heaven, and his only goal is to get you there and as many others as he can.

After college I had the privilege of backpacking Europe with some friends. At first, there were little amenities that I missed like public toilets you wouldn't have to pay for. But more than that, I missed people from home and worshiping with my church family. After a couple of months, what were passing thoughts turned into longings. As much as I loved Europe, after a while I just wanted to go home. The foreign surroundings constantly reminded me that I wasn't at home.

And when we see our lives from that perspective, then it's easier to admit . . .

God's will is always BEST.

This point takes spiritual maturity, and God blesses us with more and more of it every time we pray this part of the Lord's Prayer. It's something that Jesus understood in the Garden of Gethsemane as he prayed, **"Not my will, but yours be done"** (Luke 22:42). He knew that God's will is always best. He knew that God's goal was to get you into heaven and the only way was through the pain of the cross. Jesus died for my "my way or the highway" attitude toward God. Jesus died so that you would be in heaven. God's will is always best. And so when you find yourself questioning God's will for your life, look to the cross of Jesus and you'll have your answer. Ah, yes, dear Father, now I see.

Jesus died for my "my way or the highway" attitude toward God.

There was a man who lived almost two hundred years ago. His name was Jospeh Scriven, but you've probably never heard it and don't really need to remember it. He had to quit his studies for the military because of poor health. His girlfriend drowned the night before their wedding. His marriage plans fell apart a second time when his new fiancée died suddenly after a brief illness. Soon after, his mother found herself facing a time of terrible anxiety. The words of this man were simple. To encourage his mother, he penned a hymn. Even though you might never remember the name Joseph Scriven, you do know the words he wrote to cheer up his mother. They share the only thing to do in a life that is filled with hard times and heartache—look to Jesus. A man who had been through such sorrow understood God's will and wrote: *"What a friend we have in Jesus, all our sins and griefs to bear! What a privilege to carry everything to God in prayer! . . . Are we weak and heavy laden, cumbered with a load of care? Precious Savior, still our refuge—take it to the Lord in prayer. . . . In his arms he'll take and shield you; you will find a solace there."* May God give us the maturity to pray: "Your will be done."

Father, dear Father, your will be done. That is our hearts' one true delight. Your will is that we should have you for time and for eternity as our Father. Through Jesus, your Son, make it our will to pray boldly: Your will be done. Amen.

Give Us Today Our Daily Bread

This phrase is unique. Do you know what sets it apart? It is the only part of the Lord's Prayer that asks for physical blessings. In all the other parts of the prayer, we ask for spiritual blessings. Jesus stresses that the spiritual blessings are the most important thing. However, he still includes this phrase in his model prayer.

Daily bread probably refers to the manna that the children of Israel received in the desert as God was leading them to the Promised Land. Every morning the Israelites would go out and find this bread on the ground as their food for the day. They weren't to collect more than they needed—just enough for each day. In fact, if they tried to collect more than a day's worth, it would spoil by the next morning. God was teaching them and us that he wants us to rely on him to provide. When we pray for "daily bread," we are praying for everything we need for our body and life. When we pray, "Give us today our daily bread" . . .

God wants us to rely on him to provide.

We are praying for BREAD, not CAKE.

Notice that Jesus chooses his words carefully. He doesn't say, "Give us this day everything our hearts desire." He says, "Bread." In other words, what we *need*. We have a hard time separating wants from needs.

Can you guess what consistently makes the top

five things people look for in a home? Big closets and lots of storage. Why is that? It's because we need to have a place to store all the extra stuff we've accumulated! It's easy for us to turn "bread" into a request for "cake." And even when God gives you cake, have you ever found yourself complaining that God hasn't given you the thicker frosting you wanted? See the problem? We do well to model the wise Proverb writer: **"Give me neither poverty nor riches, but give me only my daily bread"** (Proverbs 30:8). The writer knew the dangers of plenty. We start to assume that this is what God ought to provide for us—cake, not bread. And if we don't get cake, we shake a wagging finger at God.

We live in a culture that has deified dissatisfaction. There are whole industries that exist only to make you dissatisfied with what you have . . . so that you can get something else. For us who live in such a blessed place, this section of the Lord's Prayer is a good reminder that we are really praying, "Lord, show me the difference between what I need and what I can live without. Teach me that everything I have

> *Lord, show me the difference between what I need and what I can live without.*

comes from your hand like a father giving bread to his children. Teach me to be thankful no matter if I have much or little. Continue to give me exactly what I need, even if it's not what I want. Give us today our daily bread."

We are praying for bread only for TODAY.

Sometimes it strikes me how good I have it when I evaluate the problems I have. I'm driving somewhere using my phone's GPS to get there, it's sucking battery power, and my phone prompts me to plug in. But I forgot each of my four power cords at home—ugh! Don't you hate that?! Yeah, that's a First World problem, not a Third World problem like finding clean water or food.

There was a time when Christians didn't have First World problems; they had Third World problems. They lived hand to mouth—many Christians still live that way today. In Jesus' day a man was paid at the end of the day at sundown for the work he did that day. He worked in the fields, he got his wages, he went home, and on the way he bought food to take care of his family. It doesn't take much to imagine that if a man got sick for four or five days how quickly hunger and tragedy could come to a home. He was never more than one good bout with the flu away from being hungry. And so Jesus teaches Christians then and now to trustingly pray: "Give us *today* our *daily* bread." He doesn't tell us to pray for our annual bread—he wants us to trust him every day to provide.

What about retirement? What about health insurance costs? What about my kids' braces? What about . . . ? Jesus teaches us here: "Don't worry. If I care for birds and grass, which are worth nothing, how much more will I take care of you? Aren't you worth more?" The answer is: Absolutely. You are worth Jesus' precious blood. Your Father will take care of you. Jesus says, "Trust me. Only pray like this: Give us today our daily bread."

Merciful Lord, since you are the provider of all things necessary for our bodies, fill us with trust and make us bold to pray: Give us today our daily bread. Amen.

Forgive Us Our Debts

You might be more familiar with praying this phrase using the words *trespasses* or *sins*, but Jesus here uses a monetary picture to describe our condition. Every time we sin, we go into debt to God. Satan likes to convince us that our sins aren't as bad as others so that at the end of each day we maybe rack up a couple of bucks that we owe God. It's a bold-faced lie, but even if that were true, God demands that we exit this life "debt free" to get into heaven. Colossians 3:25 says, **"Anyone who does wrong will be repaid for their wrongs, and there is no favoritism."** In other words, God is going to call in the debt at the end of your life, and if you are even $1 in the red because of sin, then hell is where you'll end up: **"The wages of sin is death"** (Romans 6:23). And here's the kicker: the Bible is clear that there is nothing you can do to pay for even one sin. Every imperfect thing you and I do, say, and even think stands in the debt column of the ledger, and there is nothing we can do to move the ledger one millimeter in a positive direction. Here's our first truth:

Forgiveness is our greatest NEED.

There was once this guy who owed a king billions of dollars. Don't stop me if you've heard this one; it's worth hearing again. The king wanted him to pay up and told him that if he didn't pay, he'd be thrown into prison until he could. How much do you make in prison again? The servant obviously couldn't pay, so do you know what the king did? He forgave the debt and let him go. This is one of Jesus' stories, and I'm assuming you figured out who the characters in it are. God is the king. We are the guy who owed an unpayable debt. Forgiveness is the one great thing we need in this life. Everything else pales in comparison. What happened to the debt? The king took the loss.

Every one of us can relate to Barabbas. Do you know who Barabbas was? He was someone sitting on death row with Jesus and the other two criminals on Good Friday morning. His debt list included murder and an untold list of other sins, not unlike your list and mine. So he was sitting in his cell, waiting to be crucified, and he heard the footsteps coming down the hall of the guard. He heard the key in the lock. The door opened and the guard said the same thing to him that God says to every one of us: "You're free. Jesus is dying in your place."

Forgiveness is the one great thing we need in this life.

And just like that, Jesus filled your greatest need. When you pray "Forgive us our debts," Jesus' *only* response is, "You are forgiven."

Forgiven people FORGIVE.

So let me finish Jesus' story from earlier. Someone just like us, who had our unpayable debts forgiven, went out and found someone that owed him a few bucks and started choking him. The king heard about it, called the guy in, and had him tortured and thrown into prison forever. Then Jesus spoke these haunting words: **"This is how my heavenly Father will treat each**

of you unless you forgive your brother or sister from your heart" (Matthew 18:35).

Have you ever held onto the debt of sin that someone else owed you, refusing to let go?

A boy was walking along a road and saw a fence that he thought might be electrified, and like little boys are wont to do, he did something dumb—he tapped his palm to the wire. He watched as his hand closed around the wire, as his muscles obeyed the irresistible impulse. Fortunately, the electricity ran in intermittent bursts, so he was able to release his grip. But for that moment, he knew what it was like to hold onto something that would kill him if he didn't let go. Jesus says that's what it's like to hold onto someone else's sin . . . eventually, it'll kill you.

"Forgive us our debts, as we also have forgiven our debtors." Please don't misunderstand Jesus. He's not saying that your forgiveness is conditioned upon whether you forgive or not. He's simply making the point that forgiven people forgive. That's just what they do. Do you struggle with that with someone—maybe he lives with you or maybe you work with her or go to school with him? Now please understand that there is a huge difference between struggling to forgive and refusing to. Maybe you have a hard time wrapping your heart around what your head already knows—this is a prayer for strength to do that! So how will you get the strength to forgive?

Forgiven people forgive.

Think of how you feel when you picture yourself

standing before God and you hear him say, "You're free. Jesus is dying in your place." Remember that the one who owes you stands right next to you. Through this prayer, may God give you strength to turn to him or her and say, "You're free. I forgive you because Jesus forgave me."

O Father, continue to erase our debts and help us forgive gladly and do good to those who wrong us. In Jesus' name make us bold to pray: Forgive us our debts, as we also have forgiven our debtors. Amen.

Lead Us Not Into Temptation

This phrase follows immediately after "Forgive us our debts." Having just prayed for forgiveness, it's only fitting that next we pray for help not to fall into sin again. And when you and I understand who we're up against in this battle against temptation, boy do we need help! Satan has more power, figuratively speaking, in the tip of his little finger than you and I have in our entire bodies. Add to that fact that he has six thousand-plus years of experience in the business of tempting, and the challenge becomes even more daunting.

He is a master at finding our Achilles' heel. Do you remember Achilles? He is a hero in Greek mythology. He was miraculously protected from wounds when his mother dipped him as a young child in the waters of the sacred River Styx. His entire body went into the river except for one of his heels by which his mother held him as she dipped him in the water. For years Achilles fought in battle after battle without injury until one day a stray arrow found the fatal soft spot of his heel and inflicted a fatal wound. Satan studies each of us, finds our Achilles' heels, and attacks us. Satan is the great tempter.

But did you notice what we just prayed? We prayed to our Father in heaven, "Lead us not into temptation." So that we don't misunderstand what we're praying, we need to first realize . . .

God cannot TEMPT us.

We're not used to saying that God can't do things. We know God is all-powerful! That means he can do whatever he wants. But that's not entirely true. There are things God can't do, tempting us being one of those things, because it would be going outside of his nature. The Bible says that God can't change (that's called God's immutability) because if he could, then he could get better. But God can't get better because he's already best. One thing that we ought to be grateful for is this: God *can't* stop loving us because God *is* love. His love led him to send Jesus for us. James says, **"When tempted, no one should say, 'God is tempting me.' For God cannot be tempted by evil, nor does he tempt anyone"** (James 1:13). So God cannot tempt us—not in the sense that we're praying about anyway.

God can't stop loving us because God is love.

The word *temptation* is actually a neutral word. In the original Greek of the Bible, it literally means "testing." It's used in two different ways in Scripture. When the Bible talks about God "tempting" us, it refers to his testing believers in order to strengthen their faith and root them deeper in the Word. Think of God asking Abraham to sacrifice his son Isaac. He was doing that to strengthen Abraham's faith, not cause him to sin.

When the Bible speaks about the devil tempting, it's always to lead us into sin and rip us away from God's Word and promises and ultimately lead us to despair. Think of Adam and Eve in the Garden of Eden. Satan's goal was to destroy them. That is his goal for you: **"Be alert and of sober mind. Your enemy the devil prowls around like a roaring lion looking for**

someone to devour" (1 Peter 5:8). One of Satan's titles in Scripture is simply Tempter. God cannot tempt us. Satan is the tempter, and so when we pray, "Lead us not into temptation," . . .

We are asking that God STRENGTHEN us to OVERCOME temptation.

Scripture speaks of the three great sources of temptation: the devil, the world, and our own sin-filled flesh. We are susceptible to all three at all times, but it's been noted that we go through stages when one is more influential than the rest. When we're young and full of energy and hormones, our sinful flesh is probably most potent with the temptations toward evil lusts like sexual sins, drunkenness, greed, and so on. As we get older, the world plays on our desire for power and ambition. No one is satisfied to be the lowest on the ladder but wants to be at the top and visible to everyone. Then the more spiritually mature we get, the devil comes in to discard God's Word the same way he approached Adam and Eve: "Did God really say that?" And he leads us to either despair that we are far too great of sinners for God to forgive us or lulls us into a false sense of security that since Jesus paid for our sins, we can do anything we want. Sometimes he gets us to despair *and* be falsely secure in the same day! We need strength to overcome!

And that strength must come from the One who overcame. Do you know the account of Jesus being tempted in the desert? Three times Satan came after him with the offer of food for a starving Jesus, a temptation to doubt for a physically weak Jesus, and a temptation for power for a scorned Jesus. All three times, Jesus overcame him with the more powerful Word of God: **"It is written: 'Man shall not live on bread alone, but on every word that comes from the mouth of God.' . . . It is also written: 'Do not put the Lord your God to the test.' . . . It is written: 'Worship the Lord your God, and serve him only'"** (Matthew 4:4,7,10). God led Jesus into the desert to be tempted so that he could do what we could never do *in our place* and so that Jesus could help us with our temptations.

Listen to the writer to the Hebrews: **"Because he himself suffered when he was tempted, he is able to help those who are being tempted"** (2:18). And again, **"We have one who has been tempted in every way, just as we are—yet he did not sin"** (4:15). You know what that means? It means we can talk to Jesus about our temptations. Most of the time we don't want to tell him. We think that if we don't tell him, maybe he won't know—but he knows! We can say to him, "How did you overcome this?"

We can talk to Jesus about our temptations.

Jesus said, **"Watch and pray so that you will not fall into temptation"** (Matthew 26:41). Jesus knows that when you're praying and asking him for help, it's harder for the devil to trick you. So not only are we asking God for strength to overcome temptation but also . . .

We are promising to FIGHT temptation.

Martin Luther said, "The devil doesn't climb the

fence where it's the highest to get to you; he climbs it where it's the lowest." In other words, know your weaknesses and flee from Satan. Scripture calls Satan a roaring lion, looking for someone to devour—don't say, "Here kitty, kitty" and try to pet him! The apostle Paul said, **"So, if you think you are standing firm, be careful that you don't fall! No temptation has overtaken you except what is common to mankind. And God is faithful; he will not let you be tempted beyond what you can bear. But when you are tempted, he will also provide a way out so that you can endure it"** (1 Corinthians 10:12,13).

Know your weaknesses and flee from Satan.

Part of the "way out" he provides is for us to use our common sense to avoid situations where we are weak. If you struggle with alcohol, a bar is not the place for you. If you struggle with pornography, a computer in a locked room is not a place for you. If you're greedy, then maybe you're not the one who should control the checkbook when offering time comes around. Playing around with temptation is like trying to run down a mountainside. There comes a time when your legs get away from you and you can no longer stop. God says, **"Resist the devil, and he will flee from you"** (James 4:7).

A story is told about a man who once asked a king how he might avoid temptation. The king replied, "I'll answer your question, but first you must take this jar of oil and carry it through the streets of the city without spilling it. If you spill so much as one drop, you will be killed." The man took the jar, walked through the city and, needless to say, was extremely careful not to spill a single drop of oil. When he returned, the king asked, "What did you see in the streets?" "Nothing," replied the man. "I was only thinking of the oil." "You've just answered your own question," the king said.

To fight temptation, your great tool is to focus all your attention on Jesus and what he's done for you, and you'll notice that the temptations fall by the wayside. See the love in his eyes that says even after you fall to temptation, "I still love you." Take a look at the wounds in his hands as he says, "I stretched these out to pay for that sin, and now I stretch them out to welcome you back." Listen as he sends you away, "I don't condemn you. Go and sin no more." May that lead you to pray, "Father, as I go, I need your help. Lead me not into temptation."

Dear Father, deliver us from the horrible temptations that would drag us away from your Word, your name, your kingdom, and your will; for we are so weak that by ourselves we will run headlong into them. Through your Son, make us bold to pray: Lead us not into temptation. Amen.

Deliver Us From the Evil One

Satan, the evil one, is responsible for the evil all around us. It's the peer pressure to sin. It's the rules that seem to bind our hands so we can't do the right thing. It's the flu we can't escape and the cancer that everyone seems to get. It's pervasive crime and tear-jerking poverty. You hate all of that? Well, there's something you have to understand about this final phrase . . .

God HATES evil too.

You see it from the very first moment that sin and evil entered this world. God walked up to find the snake smiling to himself. He looked over to see his recently corrupt creatures, Adam and Eve, pointing fingers at everyone but themselves. And God was angry, not in a sinful way but in a just and holy way. And he made a promise to send a Savior. But have you ever noticed who he addressed the first promise of a Savior to? It wasn't to the recipients of the promise; it was directed at Satan himself. You can just hear God's voice boom to make sure that snake knew his evil would be overcome: **"And I will put enmity between you and the woman, and between your offspring and hers; he** [Jesus] **will crush your head, and you will strike his heal"** (Genesis 3:15). God hates evil.

Fast-forward to a story that might make the hairs on your arm stand on end. The man was demon-possessed. He lived in the tombs. He screamed all night, every night, and cut himself with stones. Then one day he met Jesus and said, **"My name is Legion . . . for we are many"** (Mark 5:9). I dare you to think of these words tonight as you descend the basement stairs. Demons are powerful and, quite frankly, creepy. And yet, in the presence of Jesus, you see the limits of their power. Those demons knew that who-do-you-think-you-are look on God's face, that intense anger when someone so evil has touched one dear to him. They knew they weren't wanted, and they just went away. Why? Jesus told them to. That's how much stronger he is.

The devil is powerful, but he's not a god.

That's something about the evil one we need to understand. Don't think of the devil as the opposite of God. He's bad enough to be that, but he's not big enough. The devil is powerful, but he's not a god; he's not even close. He's merely another creature. By the way, hell is his prison cell, not his home.

It is to our powerful God who hates the evil one that we pray, "Deliver us from the evil one." When this God says, **"Call on me in the day of trouble; I will deliver you"** (Psalm 50:15), he means it. When he says, **"Do not fear, for I have redeemed you; I have summoned you by name; you are mine. When you pass through the waters, I will be with you; and when you pass through the rivers, they will not sweep over you"** (Isaiah 43:1,2), he'll do it.

In the greatest sense, God has ALREADY DELIVERED US from evil.

Friend, every time you witness a baptism, you get to see God answer this prayer before your very eyes and remember that he has answered it already for you. Two thousand years ago, God kept his promise to Satan in the garden. Jesus, like each one of us—spent nine months in his mother's womb, was born, and lived under God's requirements. But he kept them perfectly despite Satan's best attempts.

Then Jesus gathered up all the sins of all people. It was as if a funnel was placed over Jesus, and God took the sinful, evil world in his hand and squeezed it over that funnel. Out oozed every single drop of sin, and it filled from head to toe this Savior who loves us so much. The Bible says that he became our sin. Jesus delivered himself over to evil. He delivered himself over to sin. He delivered himself over to death. So that we need not die eternally. Then he shut the evil one's mouth forever with the sound of scraping stone as the tomb was opened on Easter morning to reveal that no one was there. Baptism connects us to that ultimate deliverance: **"Baptism now saves you also. . . . It saves you by the resurrection of Jesus Christ"** (1 Peter 3:21).

He delivered himself over to death so that we need not die eternally.

And so we pray, "Deliver us from the evil one." God responds, "I baptize you in the name of the Father and of the Son and of the Holy Spirit." Deliver us from evil?

Friends, in the greatest sense, he already has!

Heavenly Father, keep safe our bodies and souls and send the Holy Spirit to preserve our faith in Christ, which leads to eternal life. In Jesus' name make us bold to pray: Deliver us from the evil one. Amen.

Yours Forever, Amen!

"For yours is the kingdom and the power and the glory forever. Amen." These words are called the Doxology. It means a "word of praise or glory." These words have sparked an incredible amount of debate throughout the history of the church. There are some who argue strongly that they believe Jesus did not end the prayer with these words because there are ancient manuscripts that exclude them. Then there are others who argue they belong because there are many ancient manuscripts that include them and the church fathers accepted them as part of the text. How do we answer the dilemma? I don't want to be flippant, but it doesn't really matter. These words are very scriptural. King David's prayer said, **"Yours, Lord, is the greatness and the power and the glory and the majesty and the splendor, for everything in heaven and earth is yours. Yours, Lord, is the kingdom; you are exalted as head over all"** (1 Chronicles 29:11,12). Does that sound familiar? "For yours is the kingdom and the power and the glory forever. Amen." Regardless of where you come down on the debate, it's a fitting conclusion to this beautiful prayer.

The Doxology expresses PRAISE.

How can we not praise God? Joshua prayed, and the sun stood still! Elijah prayed, and the three-and-a-half-year drought came to an end! The disciples prayed, and the storm stopped! Paul and Silas prayed, and the cell doors of the jail sprung open! And that's nothing compared to what the Father, who has the kingdom, the power, and the glory forever gives you in the Lord's Prayer. In this prayer we receive pardon for the past, power in the present, and promise for the future.

Dream a little here. In a world where nothing is sacred, through this prayer, God keeps his name holy. In a world that strives to snuff out Jesus, he promises that not even the gates of hell will prevail against his kingdom. In a world that seems random, God's will is done. He provides your daily necessities; he forgives your sins and opens heaven's gates to you. He keeps temptation away and the devil at bay. Not bad for a 30-second prayer!

In this prayer we receive pardon for the past, power in the present, and promise for the future.

He does it "forever." God is eternal. That doesn't merely mean he has lived for a long, long time. As Creator of time, he lives outside of it. There is no succession of events with him. There is no yesterday or tomorrow. He lives in an eternal present. That means your birth, your life, your death, and even your glory in heaven are all *right now* to him! It's not that he will someday answer this prayer; it's that he already *is*!

What could we do but praise? In fact, that's one theory about how this part got into the prayer: that some copyist was copying this prayer and was so overcome by its magnitude that he just had to burst out in praise! And we get to call the One with the kingdom, power, and glory our Father! It takes your breath away.

This prayer has a bold beginning, and these words provide a confident end.

The Doxology expresses CONFIDENCE.

Imagine for a moment that you are the one who controls the kingdom; every power in heaven and earth is yours and you receive the glory of all. Would the world be a better place? I don't mean to offend you, but it would be a colossal mess—it would be if I had it too. Why? Because we'd use it for ourselves! It's kind of like if you won a $400 million lottery jackpot. You might use *some* of that to help others, but be honest—you'd keep most of it for your enjoyment.

God does have all of that. What does he do instead? He uses it all . . . for you. He's not out to help himself. His only concern is to help you. One of my favorite psalm verses about God's desire to give and give and give goes like this: **"The eyes of all look to you, and you give them their food at the proper time. You open your hand and satisfy the desires of every living thing"** (Psalm 145:15,16). And the greatest way the One with the kingdom, all power, and glory did that was the day he laid down on the wooden beams and the soldiers positioned his limbs as needed. Someone approached with a nail. And don't miss this next part. He didn't resist. Instead, to give you all, he opened his hand and satisfied the desires of every living thing. Jesus did everything, hanging there doing nothing . . . for you.

Jesus did everything . . . for you.

And because of that we can say, "Amen. Yes, it shall be so." Because of Jesus, *Amen* is not a question mark but an exclamation point. It's not, "Will you, Lord?" but a "You will, Lord!" This is the One who said, when you pray, pray like this: "Our Father in heaven, hallowed be your name, your kingdom come, your will be done, on earth as it is in heaven. Give us today our daily bread. And forgive us our debts, as we also have forgiven our debtors. And lead us not into temptation, but deliver us from the evil one. For the kingdom, the power, and the glory are yours now and forever." To that, we confidently say, "Amen!"

Father, dear Father, you are the King and the Lord.
You alone hold the power to give us what we ask for.
Relying on Jesus, who cancelled our sins and made
us acceptable in your sight, make us bold to pray:
It shall be so. Amen!

About The Writer

Pastor David Scharf served as a pastor in Greenville, Wisconsin, and now serves as a professor of theology at Martin Luther College in Minnesota. He has presented at numerous leadership, outreach, and missionary conferences across the country. Pastor Dave is a regular speaker on *Your* Time of Grace video devotions and a contributing writer for Time of Grace. He and his wife have six children.

About Time of Grace

Time of Grace is for people who want more growth and less struggle in their spiritual walk. The timeless truth of God's Word is delivered through television, print, and digital media with millions of content engagements each month. We connect people to God's grace so they know they are loved and forgiven and so they can start living in the freedom they've always wanted.

To discover more, please visit timeofgrace.org, download our free app at timeofgrace.org/app, or call 800.661.3311.

Help share God's message of grace!

Your generosity and prayer support take the gospel of grace to others through our ministry outreach and help them find the restart with Jesus they need.

Give today at timeofgrace.org/give or by calling 800.661.3311.

Thank you!